16 essential techniques for conquering your bipolar and Living the life you've always wanted

Jason Pegler

chipmunkapublishing
the mental health publisher

Jason Pegler

All rights reserved, no part of this publication may be reproduced by any means, electronic, mechanical photocopying, documentary, film or in any other format without prior written permission of the publisher.

>   Published by
>   Chipmunkapublishing
>   United Kingdom

http://www.chipmunkapublishing.com

Copyright © 2019 Jason Pegler

16 essential techniques for conquering your bipolar and living the life you've always wanted

In this booklet, Jason Pegler, founder of Chipmunkapublishing and the world leader in mental health empowerment, shares 16 essential techniques that will help you manage your bipolar without resorting to medication.

Drawing directly from his own experience and personal development, Jason shares such techniques as...

u _Building self esteem with ha breathing

u _The power of Neuro-linguistic Programming

u _Reprogramming your subconscious mind

u _Connecting with others

u _Setting goals and achieving them

u _How writing a book can transform your life and that of others

...and much more. You'll soon find yourself in control of your bipolar and ready to live the life you've always wanted.

"Having heard Jason Pegler speak I had the confidence to write my own story, which began as a suicide note and ended up a celebration of life. He has helped me more than anyone."

Dolly Sen

Author of four books including theThe World Is Full of Laughter
    www.chipmunkapublishing.com

16 MUST-KNOW TECHNIQUES FOR CONQUERING YOUR BIPOLAR

How you can make a paradigm shift and overcome your bipolar with the 16 principles devel-oped by a fellow bipolar and former bipolar sufferer

Jason Pegler

16 MUST-KNOW TECHNIQUES FOR CONQUERING YOUR BIPOLAR

16 MUST-KNOW TECHNIQUES FOR CONQUERING YOUR BIPOLAR

How you can make a paradigm shift and overcome your bipolar with the 16 principles devel-oped by a fellow bipolar and former bipolar sufferer

Jason Pegler

TESTIMONIALS

"We need to build on the great work that social entrepreneurs like Jason Pegler are doing."

David Cameron, Prime Minister

"Jason Pegler is inspirational to a great many people in the UK service user movement. I am amazed how he does it."

Paul Farmer, Chief Executive of Mind

"I am often asked about mental health books. A great resource is Chipmunkapublishing."

Stephen Fry

"Having heard Jason Pegler speak I had the confidence to write my own story, which began as a suicide note and ended up a celebration of life. He has helped me more than anyone."

Dolly Sen, author of four books, including The World Is Full of Laughter

"It is you putting your faith in me and publishing my book that first set me on the road to recov-ery. That is priceless."

David Stocks, RADAR, Empowerment Manager

"The positive way in which people have reacted to my book has boosted my self-esteem and empowered me. It's really pleasing to know that so many people are interested in hearing about my experiences of illness and recovery, and value what I have to say, it has confirmed to me that I have knowledge and skills that I can use to help other people, by supporting them, advocating on their behalf and hopefully empowering them – and being able to empower an-other human being is, of course, a very empowering thing."

Jason Tune author of Sex, Drugs and Northern Soul

"Seeing my book published has strengthened my resolve to carry on raising awareness of mental illness and help to reduce the associated stigma."

Judith Haire, author of Don't Mind Me

"I always say that, if I had seen someone on TV talking about body dysmorphic disorder or seen it in a magazine, I might have recognised what I myself was suffering from and sought help sooner. I suffered for fifteen years in silence. If I have been seen by just one person that felt as I did, if seeing me on TV has helped one person, then I have achieved more than any other kind of fame could hope for. A few years ago, leaving the house and being seen was my biggest fear, now, years on, I have done live TV! It really shows how my work has helped me recover."

Steve Westwood, author of Suicide Junkie

"Having Chipmunkapublishing and Jason support me whilst writing my book, and then having it published, was beyond my first intentions or dreams. I would not hesitate to encourage anyone who has had mental health experiences to consider writing a book. Thank you Chipmunkapublishing."

Linda Stoneman

"Thank you for believing in my book enough to give me a chance, I am very grateful."

Teresa Joyce

"Jason took my unusual predicament in his stride and offered much more than just a very good publishing service. He enabled me to help others being dragged along a similar path. After publishing A Cry For Help he worked tirelessly to provide me with a network of opportunities to promote my work, thus helping to raise OCD awareness. Initially, extremely nervous, I was surprised by the positive feedback due to Jason's campaign. An article in That's Life magazine and the local newspaper inspired a number of people, totally uneducated regarding OCD, to purchase my accounts and fathom my actions. Local people started to grasp the realities of OCD. The attitude of condemnation was very gradually replaced, in many cases, by sympathetic understanding.

Jason, while providing a rock of support, toiled to widen the net of opportunity. National news-papers and television programmes climbed aboard. The Trisha Goddard Show gave me a greater platform to discuss OCD. Encouraged by Jason, I strived to help people understand the condition and, where needed, seek professional help. I had an issue with my 'intrusive thoughts', feeling embarrassed and totally isolated, opting to go to jail rather than admit to having them."

Stephen Drake, author of A Cry For Help

"Thank you very much for the book. I cannot tell you how much I value it. I was in a permanent tantrum before you published me and now I've become quite positive and happy."

Simon Rhys Shaw

"Chipmunkapublishing is an invaluable service to so many. Being able to 'tell my story' and be respected for my work as well as have my experiences validated has been an integral and instrumental part of my own healing process. Thank you for helping so many find their wings and fly."

Clare Wilson

Jason Pegler

INTRODUCTION

I was first diagnosed with manic depression at the age of 17.

The moment I realised I had a mental illness I had an epiphany, a mission and a dream. Ever since then, my goal in life is to help others and make the world a better place. To do this, I founded Chipmunkapublishing – a platform to allow people to tell the truth about how people with mental health issues are treated by society, the mental health system, the state and the status quo. I want others to follow in my footsteps and help Chipmunkapublishing break down the taboos surrounding mental health once and for all.

This book contains sixteen of the most important discoveries I have made in the management of my own bipolar – techniques that helped me successfully go off medication and enjoy every minute of my life. They will help you do the same, without resorting to drugs and medication.

I hope these techniques inspire you to take charge of your own bipolar and that I will have the opportunity to help you tell your own story in the future.

Good luck!

Jason Pegler

Owner and Founder Chipmunkapublishing

Jason Pegler

1. Making Decisions

The first thing you have to do to conquer your bipolar is to be prepared to take massive action in your life. If you do not, then you will not progress and be a victim of the law of diminishing intent. If you decide to act instead of hesitating then you will be amazed at the opportunities for turning your life around that are out there.

2. Goal setting

Writing down specific goals is an essential part of getting better. You have to write your goals down every day in a certain, very specific, way. Feel free to change your goals at any time if you want. They are flexible. The more goals you write each day the more you will accomplish.

Write your goals in the first person and in the present tense. They can be as ambitious as you want, although you have to believe that they are possible. Aim to write at least 10-15 goals half an hour before you sleep. Your subconscious mind will process them and you will be ready for action when you wake up. Feel free to add more goals in the morning and throughout the day. Carrying your goals with you on your mobile phone in the 'notes' section makes keeping them with you at all times easy.

Most people will never write their goals down. If you can write yours down you will stay fo-cused. Make sure that your goals are believable as well. If it helps you can add a date and even a year to your goals. The more goals that you write down every day, the more you will accomplish. Do not neglect any achievement, no matter how small – each one is a cause for celebration.

3. Writing as catharsis

Writing can be a cathartic process. Writing one's autobiography is a deeply personal process. When I wrote A Can of Madness I poured my heart out on the page. It was extremely intense but, overall, an extremely rewarding experience. Writing saved my life and enabled me to put my manic depression behind me once and for all. I urge you to trust the writing process and just let the things in your head just pour out onto the page like I did.

You may already harbor dreams of being a writer, or you may have never tried, or even con-sidered, writing before. Whatever your previous writing experience, you will be amazed at the results.

Write your title first and then get everything you can down in the first person, writing positive words. If it helps, start with some positive writing prompts, such as "I am celebrating my bipolar because..." Be sure to have a happy middle and end as well. Aim to write 2000 words a day (like Stephen King does) and do not stop until you have reached that target.

Try to avoid overthinking the process – just let your emotions flow naturally onto the page. You can go back and edit your work afterwards for the sake of clarity (check for typos, etc.) but make sure you avoid any drastic rewrites.

If you follow this technique then you will have the first draft of your autobiography finished in no time. Not only will this be a wonderfully cathartic process for you, sharing your story by publishing your work can be a huge source of inspiration to fellow bipolars, who may assume they have to suffer in silence. Never assume no-one would be interested in your story – each of us has something unique to share with the world and writing a book is the best way to do it.

4. Building self esteem

Try this exercise for building your self esteem. You can do this in a number of ways. Hold your right bicep with your left hand and feel your emotional thermostat. As soon as you wake up in the morning and before you go to bed at night have a big smile on your face and force yourself to smile for 5 minutes. Then say "I like myself" as fast as you can, then "I love myself and I love everyone else" as quickly as you can. Tell yourself that you are going to be the happiest person in the world.

At the same time clench every muscle in your body starting with your feet, then your legs, then your arms, then your six-pack (come on, you know it's in there somewhere!), then your fingers and toes. Clench every muscle in your body for 2 minutes and smile while you are doing it. Start with your feet, then move up to your legs, your stomach, your back, your arms and your head. Keep smiling.

Doing these exercises last thing at night, first thing in the morning and whenever else you feel like it throughout the day will give you tremendous self esteem and will make it impossible for you to feel unwell.

When you force yourself to be happy in your actions, voice, mind, heart and body it really works – there'll never be any need to feel unhappy again.

5. Be positive

Act in a positive way all of the time. The way you feel and act can change in a heartbeat. See the world as a wonderful place. Be grateful for everything good in your life and good in the world.

Avoid watching the news for seven days. Put your hand on your heart and promise to not moan about anything for seven days. If you find yourself beginning to moan, then stop... smile... be positive and willingly start the seven days again.

You will be amazed at how different you feel and you will also be amazed at how the people around you in your life act as well. Your positivity will rub off on them. If not, then change the circle of people you hang around with where possible and invite more positive people into your life. Don't be afraid to lose acquaintances if they are a persistent negative influence.

6. Reaching out to other people

Share everything positive that you learn or do in your life and celebrate the successes of oth-ers. The more you can reach out to others and connect with them the more you are pushing your bipolar aside and bringing out the real you. If you feel nervous about connecting with others, say "I like myself, I like myself " when you are on your own for 2 minutes as fast as you can. The more you like yourself the more confident you will feel and the easier it will be to connect with other people.

Connecting with your fellow bipolars can be a wonderful experience. We often allow ourselves to believe that we are the only ones dealing with our particular mental health issues, leading to feelings of isolation and loneliness. This is a mistake. By sharing our experiences and hearing from those who have learnt to manage their bipolar, it becomes clear that we needn't allow ourselves to be prisoners and that we can live the kind of lives we have always dreamed of.

Try reading some of the books written by other bipolars. They could easily be just the thing you need to inspire you and help you reconnect with others.

7. Understand the difference between beliefs and rules

Where you focus on in life is where you end up. Take the decision now to focus on the positive or even force a positive image, action, mindset upon you, your life and everything that you are going to do. Choose to become a winner and not a victim. Put your blame list aside once and for all. You will then realise that the world is a wonderful place and find that, when you have a positive outlook on life, the universe is a real positivity magnet.

Remember, many of the 'rules' we allow to hold us back are in fact 'beliefs'; they have no ob-jective reality outside of our own minds. Once you understand this and start working through your own library of restrictive 'rules', you'll be amazed how many of them you will be able to let go of. By replacing them with positive, inspiring beliefs, your whole outlook on life will be transformed.

The more you can focus on this positive energy and the positive aspects of life, the more your bipolar will vanish and you'll find your old self replaced by the real, upgraded version of your-self that you always dreamt of.

Look yourself in the mirror everyday and tell yourself that you love yourself, i.e. say "I love my-self! I love my outlook! I love my beliefs!" Say it over and over again with your hand on your heart until you feel a transformation, where your whole body enters a peak state.

8. Stop procrastinating

It's easy to fall into the trap of procrastination; making excuses for everything that is wrong in our lives and placing the blame on forces beyond our control.

Focus on the most important things every day, all of the time. If something seems particularly different, then imagine eating the ugliest frog in front of you and getting that out of the way as soon as you wake up.

This way the day will get easier and easier. The harder you are on yourself in life, the easier life will be for you. This is because the more you push yourself, the more skills you develop and the more ability you have to manage whatever life has in store.

9. Let go of limiting beliefs

Choose to let go of limiting beliefs as soon as they appear and immediately replace them with the greatest things you can imagine. Start by writing down your most important values – the things that matter most to you in life – in no particular order. Then go back and put them in or-der of importance.

Once you have your top 5, start writing 50-100 things that you would really like. Aim big! Imag-ing being in the future, where you have everything you desire – millions of pounds, a happy family, good health etc. Then, once you have your 50/100 outcomes, go through each one and give each of them a time period (1, 3, 5 or 10 years) for when you'd like to achieve them.

Once you have done that, go back and choose the 5 most important to you. Read these every day and re-do your top 5 if you wish (or redo the whole exercise once a month to keep yourself on track). Write down a vivid description of the person you will have to become to achieve your goals. Include at least 20 words of description and reread the list every day for the next 12 months. You will soon find yourself well on the way to becoming that person.

It's a great feeling when you look back at these lists and realise how much you have already accomplished!

10. Mastering inner confidence through ha breathing

Originating in Hawaii, ha breathing is an excellent tool for increasing your inner confidence. With a little practice each day it will help you develop greater self-confidence by building up air energy that can be redirected round the body.

Sit down somewhere quiet each day and do some ha breathing for 10 minutes in the morning and 10 minutes at night. Move into a place where you will not be disturbed. Take a deep breath in through the nose, filling your lungs completely. Then exhale through the mouth, loudly whispering the word 'Haaaa'. This will give you the confidence and energy to achieve anything you want to throughout the day.

11. Self-awareness and realisation

Learn to know your mind and know your body and soul. Be aware when you are self-manifesting your bipolar and negative thoughts. Make a conscious decision to be positive. If you feel yourself slipping into a negative mindset, then stand up straight and tall and tell yourself that you are special – make a conscious decision to change your attitude.

Even small changes in outlook have a cumulative effect over time: if you make a one-degree shift in your attitude once a day then it is amazing how far you will have progressed after a few weeks, a few months, 6 months and a year or two.

12. Shifting paradigms

Imagine that bipolar is just a social construct and stop feeling sorry for yourself or blaming an-yone else for it. Take 100% of the responsibility for your situation in life and where you are at this moment in time.

Stand up straight. Look in the mirror. Force yourself to smile. Say to yourself repeatedly "I am happy" for two minutes and keep smiling as you are saying it. Then continue for another two minutes, saying, as fast as you can, "I choose to feel better every day". Then put your hands up in the air and celebrate for 5 minutes, jumping up and down saying "Yes! I am better!" whenever you catch your breath. Have some water after you have finished and sit up straight. You will feel great.

13. Focus

Stay focused. Focus on the most important task in front of you at any given time. Complete tasks as much as you can before moving on to the next task. Most people complete 95% of a task then move on to the next task. It is better to finish something and do it badly than to give up and not finish it at all.

If you focus on completing tasks rather than abandoning them, you will soon have an impres-sive list of accomplishments to look back on – a great cure for any periods of low self-esteem.

14. Get enough quality sleep

Get enough quality sleep – at least 7 hours per night.

Do not have any caffeine after 2pm. Avoid alcohol completely. Do not do strong physical exer-cise 3 hours before going to sleep. Do not watch the television one hour before going to bed. Do not use the computer 30 minutes before going to bed. When you go to sleep, focus on loosening every part of your body beforehand.

Talk to yourself and say "I am going to have a great sleep tonight". If you find yourself repeat-edly waking up, go through the same process again and again and imagine yourself having a great sleep. You'll soon be enjoying quality sleep every night and feel better throughout the day as a result.

15. Get into and use NLP techniques

Study Neuro-linguistic Programming (NLP). NLP is the art of modelling excellence invented by Dr. Richard Bandler and John Grinder in the 1970's. It is a unique form of modelling excellence that focuses on identifying and altering patterns of behaviour. The goal is increased self-awareness, improved communication and the ability to positively affect your own mental and emotional state.

This is a must for anyone with bipolar. Studying NLP will give you the tools to make your bipo-lar an insignificant part of your life. It is the ultimate secret weapon and booster for any bipolar sufferer. Read about it, understand it and implement it. I have been using NLP techniques for 10 years and they have really helped me in the management of my own bipolar.

Through NLP you can identify negative patterns of behaviour and change them for the better, affecting lasting, positive change in your outlook on life.

16. Reprogram your subconscious mind

Your subconscious mind is 100 times more powerful than your conscious mind. What's more, you can influence it by sending positive signals to it. The more you give it positive signals the more power you have to distinguish your bipolar manifestations and download the positive attitude that you envisage. Where you focus on in life is where you end up. So start reprogramming your mind and make sure you're heading where you want to be.

Write down 100 things that if they happened would make you extremely happy. Write about your relationships, family, health, finances, spirituality and emotions... any positive changes you would like to see in your life.

Each night before you go to bed, read them out loud. Then, when you are asleep, the positive messages that you have sent to yourself will give you happier dreams and put you in a better mood when you wake up every day. Refine the list on a daily basis and turn your subconscious mind to your advantage.

Conclusion

I hope that the techniques in this book prove useful in managing your own bipolar and that you feel sufficiently inspired to put pen to paper and start chronicling your experiences.

Remember, once you start looking at the world with a positive attitude and connecting with those around you, your bipolar will lose its hold on you and you will be ready to go out and make a positive difference in the world.

Never be afraid to enjoy life! Life is a precious jewel that we all take for granted at some time or other. Enjoy the journey as well as the destination. Learn to appreciate every single day. Have gratitude for everything that is good in your life and your positive karma will impact on other people, helping to make the world a better place.

Let me tell you a little more about Chipmunkapublishing and how we can help you become a published author and share your experiences with the world...

ABOUT JASON PEGLER

Jason Pegler is the world leader in mental health empowerment and winner of the 2005 New Statesman's Young Social Entrepreneur of the Year Award. Since 2001 he has dedicated his life to giving a voice to people with mental illness, helping them tell their stories and breaking down the stigma attached to mental health.

He is a published author, having written the critically acclaimed autobiography on living with manic depression, entitled A Can of Madness, described as "A brilliant memoir of mania" by Stephen Fry. He is the owner and founder of Chipmunkapublishing, the Mental Health Publisher, which has published over 600 authors and over 600 paperbacks within its first 10 years.

He regularly appears on National BBC television and National Radio. He has done interviews in Australia, New Zealand, United States, Jerusalem, Ireland, Spain and featured on ITV, Na-tional BBC television and radio over 100 times.

ABOUT CHIPMUNKA

Mental health books give a voice to writers with mental illness around the world. At Chipmun-kapublishing we raise awareness of mental health and the stigma surrounding mental health problems by encouraging society to listen. We are documenting mental health literature as a genre so history does not forget the survivors and carers of people with mental illness and disabilities.

Most of our publications are written by people with mental health issues. We also give a voice to family members of people with mental health issues and many other disabilities. Titles in-clude autobiographies/memoirs, fiction, poetry, film scripts, plays, books of lyrics, anthologies, stories written by carers, self help books, academic works and more.

We are a unique social enterprise focused on publishing both factual and creative literature. We want to reduce the humiliation that people with "mental illness" feel by being the main publisher of the mental health literary genre. We give people with mental illness a voice so that they can have the opportunity and positive mindset needed to lead better lives and hopefully full recoveries, or a least a deeper understanding and acceptance of what they have experienced.

We also publish people who have learnt to live with their experiences, so their books can in-spire fellow sufferers.

Do not let your children grow up misunderstanding people with mental health issues. Let's improve society so that mental health artists can empower people with mental health issues to be equal in society. Then they can shape their future and help others.

We work with governments, health services, the media, mental health organisations, charities and private businesses to successfully publish and promote literature that encourages a posi-tive attitude towards mental health issues. Chipmunkapublishing aims to break down the stig-ma surrounding mental illness once and for all.

Chipmunkapublishing gratefully acknowledges the support of Arts Council England.

www.chipmunkapublishing.com

A SPECIAL INVITATION FROM CHIPMUNKA

I would like to invite you to a special seminar, where you can learn more techniques for con-quering your bipolar and also learn more about becoming a Chipmunka author. You'll spend three days learning more about such topics as:

- The power of writing and how it can transform your life

- Advice on product development and submitting your own manuscript to Chipmunka

- Generating worldwide publicity to make sure people hear your story

- Developing your niche and the principles of successful marketing

- An introduction to mental health empowerment technology

- Techniques and exercises for cultivating a positive attitude

- An introduction to Neuro-linguistic Programming techniques

I hope to see you there and put you on the path to sharing your story with the world.

To find out more, go towww.chipmunkahealth.com

Jason Pegler

www.ingramcontent.com/pod-product-compliance
Lightning Source LLC
Chambersburg PA
CBHW070210100426
42743CB00013B/3125